PROFESSIONAL ETHICS, ACCOUNTABILITY OF LAWYERS & BAR BENCH RELATION

POOJA AGARWAL

Made with ❤ on the Notion Press Platform
www.notionpress.com

Contents

Preface

POOJA AGARWAL

This book primarily covers legal professional ethics and court etiquette relevant to the duty of a lawyer in the major legal systems of the world. It emphasizes the point that lawyers must not only practice their craft with absolute integrity but should also be well behaved and civil to each other, the courts and other court users. Lawyers are first and foremost officers of the court; it is their duty to assist the court come to a proper and just determination of the issues in dispute, serving before the court. A lawyer's duty to the court includes candour, honesty, and fairness. Lawyers, especially in an adversarial system, are required to act professionally with scrupulous fairness and integrity and to aid the court in promoting the cause of justice. There is an obligation on a lawyer not to take on a case in circumstances where the lawyer is plainly unqualified for the complexity of the task or has an inadequate knowledge of the area of law concerned. It is the duty of every lawyer to assist the judge by simplification and concentration and not to advance a multitude of ingenious arguments in the hope that one of the many arguments will win the day. Litigants and their lawyers are not entitled to the uncontrolled use of a trial judge's time. Litigants are only entitled to so much of the trial judge's time as is necessary for the proper determination of the relevant issues. Without this assistance from lawyers, the courts are unlikely to succeed in their endeavour to administer justice in a timely and efficient manner.

1

Origin and Development of Legal Profession

Origin

In India, the Legal profession originated during the British Rule. There is no evidence of the existence of legal Profession before that i.e. During the Hindu Rule and Mughal Dynasty period. During that period, the administration of justice was in the hands of the King and the Kings court was treated as the highest court of the country.

There is no appeal against the order of the King. Persons disobeyed the King's order was charged with sedition. During that period the King was respected as the representative of God who was sent by the God to render justice to the people.

In the King's court the plaintiff has to represent his case personally and thereafter the King will hear the other side. To assist and advice and the King in the administration of justice there was a council of ministers and a group of educationalists.

During Britisher's Period

The East India Company which started its business in India, during 16th century slowly started capturing important cities in India and they started administering those areas under their control. They have created company courts and those courts were headed by persons having no legal knowledge. And persons having no legal knowledge were allowed to practice in the court.

The first time in India, the legal profession was recognized and regulated by the Charter Act of 1774. This Act has permitted the English lawyers to practice in the Supreme Court of Calcutta.

Later on in 1801, the English lawyers were allowed to practice in the Madras Supreme Court and in the year 1823 they were allowed to practice in the Bombay Supreme Court, but Indian Lawyers were not allowed to Practice in those courts. (In 1826 these 3 Supreme Courts were abolished and, in that place, High Courts were Created).

In 1865, the Special Rights Act has conferred the right to the Madras, Bombay and Calcutta High Courts to frame rules for the recognition of Advocates and for preparing the Advocates roll.

In 1879, the Legal Practioner's Act has conferred the similar power to the other High court Were allowed to practice in that high court. As per this Act Persons studied Law in England Were called as Advocates and persons studied Law in India were called as "Vakils". The "Vakils" were not allowed to practice before the High Courts.

In 1923, an Advocates Committee was constituted under the leadership of Sir. Edward to study the legal profession and to make suitable recommendations to improve the legal profession. This committee has recommended for the creation of Bar Councils in each High Court and allowing the "Vakils" to practice before the High Court.

Accepting the recommendation Bar Council Act was passed in 1926. This Act was paved the way for the creation of Bar Councils in each High Courts. But the Bar Council was not empowered to enroll Advocates, that power was retained with the High Courts. The function of the Bar Council was only advisory and the rules and regulations made by the Bar Council shall be brought into force only after the concurrence from the High Court.

After Independence

After Independence in the year 1951 an Advocates Committee was constituted under the chairmanship of Justice

C.R. Das to study the problems in the legal profession and make suitable suggestions to remedy such problems. This committee has made the following recommendations.

1. All India level, one Bar Council namely Bar Council of India and in each state, State Bar Council should be created.
2. Power to enroll Advocates and disciplinary power against the Advocates should be entrusted with the Bar Council.
3. Advocates should be allowed to practice throughout India without any discrimination.

The fifth Law Commission also scrutinized these recommendations and recommended for the implementation of these recommendations. Accepting these recommendations, the Central Govt. passed the Advocates Act in the year 1961 giving suitable provision for creation of Bar Councils and the Bar Councils are entrusted with the power of regulating the legal profession.

2

Salient Features of Advocates Act

The Advocate's Act was passed by the Parliament in the year 1961. Following are some of the important salient features.

1. The Act has consolidated all the existing law on legal profession.
2. The Act has made provision for the creation of Bar Council of India at the Central level and State bar Councils in each state.
3. The Act has made the provision for the preparation of common roll of Advocates throughout India.
4. It empowers Advocates whose name is in the common roll to practice in all the courts in India.
5. The difference between the Advocates and Vakil is abolished and all those who practice law is called as Advocates.
6. Provisions are made to confer the status as Senior Advocate for those Advocates who poses extraordinary knowledge in the field of law.

7. It has conferred autonomous status to the Bar Councils.

SCOPE OF THE INDIAN ADVOCATES ACT, 1961

The Bar Council of India, under this act, can make rules on the matters like the election of other Bar council members or the election of the president and vice president. If there is any dispute regarding the election of any sought or the validity of these elections, the decision of the Bar Council will be final.

3

Bar Council of India

Constitution

The following persons are the members of the Bar Council of India.

1. One member from each State Bar Councils. He will be elected by the members of the respective State Bar Councils.
2. Attorney General of India-Ex Officio member.
3. Solicitor General of India-Ex officio member.

Ex-officio members will continue as members so long as they hold the offices of Attorney General and Solicitor General posts. The other members will continue as members so long they are continuing as members of the State Bar Council.

Powers

Bar Council of India is empowered with the following powers.

1. It is a body corporate.
2. It is legal persons having the autonomous status.

3. It has a common seal and perpetual succession.
4. It can do the following things in its own name. Buying and selling properties, entering into agreements, Filing cases etc.
5. Transfer the name of the Advocate from one state roll to another state roll on his application.
6. It can constitute executive committee, disciplinary committee, legal aid committee etc.
7. To hear and decide appeal, review and revision against the orders of the disciplinary committee of the State Bar Council.
8. Frame rules relating to day-to-day administration.

Functions

S.7 of the Advocates Act empowers the Bar Council of India to perform the following functions.

1. Frame the rules relating to the professional ethics.
2. Frame the rules of procedure to be followed by the disciplinary committee of the State Bar Councils and the Bar Council of India.
3. Protect the rights and the privileges of the Advocates.
4. Encourage legal reforms.
5. Decide the repute relating to professional misconduct which is transferred from the disciplinary committee of the State Bar Council to the Bar Council of India.
6. Decide the appeal against the disciplinary committee of the State Bar Council.
7. Supervise the functions of the State Bar Council.
8. Prescribe the syllabus of the law course in consultation with the State Bar Councils and the universities.
9. Inspect the universities for the purpose of giving recognition to the law degrees of the universities.

10. Spend the Funds of the Bar Council of India for the proper purposes.
11. Conduct elections for the purpose of electing its members.
12. Allow the persons studied abroad to practice in India.
13. Do all other acts which are necessary for the effective implementation of the above said function.

4

State Bar Council

Constitution

S.3 of the Advocates Act empowers for the creation of State bar councils for every state. Number of members of the Bar Council varies from state to state, depending upon the number of Advocates on the State roll.

1. If the number of Advocates in the state roll is less than 5000, then the number of Bar Council members are 15.
2. If the number of Advocates are 5000 to 10000 then the number of Bar Council members are 20.
3. If the number of Advocates are more than 10000 then the number of bar Council members are 25.
4. Members are elected by the Advocates whose names are there in the state roll by a single transferrable vote. The members hold office for a period of 5 years.

The Advocate General of the Concerned State is an ex-officio member of the State Bar Council. So long as he is holding the office as Advocate General he can act as the member of the Bar Council.

Powers

The State Bar Council is empowered with the following powers.

1. It is body corporate.
2. It is a legal body having the autonomous status.
3. It has a common seal and perpetual succession.
4. It can do the following things in its own name. Buying and selling properties, entering into agreements, Filing cases.
5. It can constitute executive committee etc.
6. It can frame rules and regulations relating to day-to-day administration.

Functions

Advocates Act empowers the State Bar Council to do the following functions.

1. Enroll the qualified persons as Advocates.
2. Prepare the Advocates roll.
3. Take disciplinary action for professional misconduct.
4. Protect the rights and privileges of the Advocates.
5. Encourage law reforms. For this purpose, it organizes seminars, talks and publish journals.
6. Constitute executive committee, enrolment committee, disciplinary committee, legal aid committee etc.
7. Manage the funds of the Bar Council.
8. Conduct the election for electing the members of the State Bar Council.
9. Prepare legal aid programmers and allot separate funds for the implementation of such schemes.
10. Prepare Schemes for helping the poor Advocates and allot separate funds for the implementation of such schemes.

11. Grant recognition to the law colleges.
12. Do all other acts which are necessary for the effective implementation of the above said functions.

5

Qualification & Disqualification Prescribed for Enrolment

Qualification

S.24 of the Advocates Act prescribes the following qualifications for a person to enroll as an Advocate.

1. He must be a citizen of India.
2. He must have completed 21 years of age.
3. He must have passed 3 years law course (regular study from the university after graduation) or 5 years integrated Law course after 10 +2. If the law degree is from any Foreign University, then it must be a recognized degree, for the Advocates Act by the Bar Council of India.
4. He should pay an enrolment fee as may be prescribed by the State Bar Council.

5. He must fulfill such other conditions as may be prescribed by the State Bar Council for the purpose of enrolment.

No upper age limit for enrolment is fixed in the Advocates Act.

So, after 21 years at any age one can enroll as an Advocate

Disqualification

The following persons are disqualified to enroll as an Advocate (S.24A).

1. A person convicted for an offence involving moral turpitude.
2. A person convicted for an offence under untouchability (offences) Act, 1955.
3. A person dismissed or removed from government service on any charge involving moral turpitude.

The disqualification ceases to have effect after the period of two years of his release from jail or dismissal from service.

There is no disqualification for a person found guilty in the above said cases and who has been given benefit under the provisions of the Probation of Offenders Act, 1958.

If an application for the enrolment is refused on any one of the above grounds of disqualification, the State bar Council has intimated that fact stating the name, address, reasons for refusal to all other State Bar Councils, thereby he shall be prevented from applying to the other State Bar Councils for Enrolment.

A person cannot be permitted to carry on other profession along with legal profession. So, a person with a law degree is carrying on the other profession is disqualified to enroll as an Advocate (**Hani Raj L. Chulani V. Bar council of Maharashtra**).

A full-time salaried law officer is not entitled to enroll as an Advocate [**Sathish Kumar Sharma V. Bar Council of Himachal Pradesh (AIR 2001 SC 509)**].

6

Supreme Court Advocates

The Supreme Court rules of practice classifies the Advocates into three categories. They are

(i)Ordinary Advocates

(ii) Senior Advocates

(iii) Advocates on Record

Senior Advocates

S.16 of the Advocates Act classifies the Advocates into two types namely, Senior Advocates and other Advocates.

The Supreme Court or a High Court shall designate an Advocate with his consent, as Senior Advocate, if the court is of the opinion that by virtue of his ability, standing at the Bar or special knowledge or experience in the law, he deserves such distinction. It is an honor and privilege conferred on an Advocate.

By virtue of the pre-eminence which a senior Advocate enjoys in the profession, they carry the greatest responsibilities and they should act as a model to the junior members of the profession. A senior Advocate more or less occupies a position like a Queen 's Counsel in England next after the Attorney General, the Solicitor General and the State Advocate General.

Order-IV Rule-2 regarding the 1966 deals with the rules regarding the designating an Advocate as a Senior Advocate in the Supreme Court and their conditions of practice. Each High court has framed their own rules of procedures for designating an Advocate as Senior Advocate.

The Bar Council of India has prescribed the following restrictions in the matter of practice of a Senior Advocate.

1. A senior Advocate shall not file a Vakalatnama or a memo of appearance or pleading or application in any court or tribunal or before any person or authority mentioned in S.30 of the Act.
2. A Senior Advocate in the Supreme Court shall not appear without an Advocate on record in the Supreme Court.
3. A Senior Advocate in the High Court shall not appear Without an Advocate of the state roll.
4. He shall not accept instructions to draft pleading or affidavits, or to do any drafting work of an analogous nature.
5. He shall not undertake conveyancing work of any kind what so ever.
6. He shall not directly accept a case from a client or instructions from his client to appear in any court or tribunal.
7. He is free to make concessions or give undertakings in course of arguments on behalf of his client on instructions from the junior Advocate.

When an Advocate is designated as a Senior Advocate, the registrar of the Supreme court or the High court, as the case may be, shall communicate it to all the High courts and the secretary to the State Bar Council and the Bar Council of India. In the communication, the Name of the Advocate and the date on which he was designated as the Senior Advocate should be mentioned.

Advocate on Record

An Advocate should have the following qualifications to become as an Advocate on Record.

1. He must have completed 4 years of service as Advocate.
2. In addition to the four years of Service as Advocate he should work for one year with an Advocate On Record, who has more than 10 years of service.
3. He should pass the Advocate On Record test conducted by the Supreme Court.

The test will be conducted on the following four subjects for hundred marks each namely (i)Supreme Court Rules of practice and procedures, (ii) Drafting and Pleading (iii) Accountancy for the lawyers and (iv) Leading cases. To pass this test one should get minimum 50% in each subject and in aggregate minimum 60%. i.e., Totally 240 marks.

The Successful Advocates will be recognized as Advocate On Record by the Supreme Court and their name will be entered in a separate register maintained for this purpose. Only Advocates on Record alone is entitled to file cases in the Supreme Court. Every year they should submit their annual income and expenditure account to the Supreme Court.

If an Advocate on Record is selected as the Senior Advocate, then his name will be removed from the register of the Advocate on Record and will be put in the register of the Senior Advocate.

Advocates Roll

According to S.17 of the Advocates Act, every State Bar Council shall prepare and maintain a roll of Advocates. It shall contain two parts. First part containing the list of Senior Advocates and the second part containing the other Advocates.

When more than one Advocate is enrolled in a single day, based on their seniority in age their name will be entered in order. In the Advocates roll the following details should be mentioned.

The name, Date of Birth, Permanent address, details about his education, the place where he is interested to practice etc.

A person cannot enroll himself as an Advocate in more than one Bar Council. A person whose name is registered in one state Roll can transfer his name in other State Roll on genuine grounds by an application to the Bar Council of India. If there is no genuine reason for transfer or any disciplinary proceedings are pending against him then transfer application will be rejected.

The State Bar Council should send an authenticated copy of the Advocates Roll whenever the new Advocates are included or names are removed from the roll.

7

Amicus Curiae

Amicus Curiae means 'friend of the court'. He is the person who is voluntarily or on an invitation of the court gives his opinion to the Court on a question of law in which the court is doubtful.

Amicus Curiae is not an Advocate retained by any of the parties to the dispute. He is altogether a stranger to the case. By virtue of his standing in the profession and the Experience in the particular field of law the court may request to give his opinion on a particular issue. His views are only an information or a suggestion to the court. An amicus curiae can express his views only with the leave of the court. Normally he is not entitled to any remuneration of such work.

8

Lawyers Privileges

Privilege means special kind of right. An Advocate being the officer of the court and belonging to the noble profession enjoys certain privileges inside and outside the court. The practice of law itself is a privilege conferred on lawyers. It is not open to anyone who wishes to practice law, only lawyers alone can practice law.

Following are some of the privileges.

1. A Lawyer has the privilege to represent his clients in the court and tribunals.
2. A lawyer while going to the court to attend the case or while returning from the court is exempted from arrest under civil process.
3. A lawyer has a privilege of becoming judge, Attorney general, Solicitor General, Advocate General and government councils.
4. Since he is fighting for the justice, he is respected next to God.

9

Seven Lamps of Advocacy

Justice 'Abbot Parry' qualifies the following qualities as "Seven Lamps of Advocacy".

They are (i) Honesty (ii) Courage (iii) Industry (iv)wit, (v)Eloquence, (vi) Judgement and (vii) Fellowship.

1. ***Honesty:*** Honesty is the most important quality that an advocate should possess. His thoughts words and deeds should have sincere co- relation to each other with genuineness. An Advocate should be dependable reliable to everyone who seeks his advice and services. The uprightness, integrity and honesty of the Advocate will increase his reputations and respect in the society.
2. ***Courage:*** It is the duty of an Advocate to fearlessly uphold the interest of his client by all fair means without fear of any unpleasant consequences to himself or any other person. It is the knowledge and the skill of the Advocate that gives him the necessary courage and confidence to present the case fearlessly and to uphold the interest of the client. The knowledge and the skill

can be acquired and developed by mastery of facts, mastery of laws, mastery in drafting and presentations of convincing arguments.

3. ***Industry:*** It means hard work. Hard works is absolutely necessary for an Advocate. His knowledge of law should be up to date. He shall never be ignorant of the current law in force. He shall get acquainted with the latest law by systematic study. If one ignores the law, the law will also ignore him. That is why it is said that "law is the jealous mistress".
4. ***Wit:*** Judges and lawyers have to deal with a variety of serious and important matters affecting life and liberty of the people. So constant clash between them is common. Anxiety for a favorable verdict on the part of the lawyers; and perpetual worry for the pursuit of the truth on the part of the judges generate strain and tension. Occasional wit and humor, provoking a smile or laughter will help them to ease the tension, and refresh themselves to sharpen their brain for the effective discharges of the duties.
5. ***Eloquence:*** Eloquence means the fluency, force and style of using the language. Strong vocabulary is one of the powerful weapons which an Advocate should possess. Words are his keys of thoughts. Strong vocabulary gives him assurance, build his self-confidence and build his personality. Words must be employed with eloquence. The art of persuasive and impressive speaking will give the desired result in his favor.
6. ***Judgement:*** It means the ability to come to a sensible conclusion and make wise decisions at the relevant time in the proper way. It is on the basis of these conclusions he should employ the necessary facts and the techniques in the case which he is engaged. This quality is necessary

from the beginning of filing the case till its final disposal. An Advocate must always anticipate all the possible moves of the other side and must develop the necessary presence of mind, alertness and tact to cope with any awkward situation of difficulty that may arise in the case.

7. ***Fellowship:*** In legal profession, one Advocate fights with another Advocate for justice before the learned judge. There may be controversies and contradictions in their contention relating to the case, but that shall never affect the fellowship. The Advocates should refer the opposite party's Advocate as "Learned Friend" and the judge should be referred as "Learned Judge". In order to maintain the fellowship, the Bar Council of India has laid down certain rules to be observed as the duty to colleagues.

10

Panchsheel of the Bar

Panchsheel refers to the following five qualities.

They are (i) Honesty (ii) industry (iii) justice (iv) Service and (v) Philosophy.

1. ***Honesty:*** Honesty is the most important quality that an advocate should possess. His thoughts words and deeds should have sincere co- relation to each other with genuineness. An Advocate should be dependable reliable to everyone who seeks his advice and services. The uprightness, integrity and honesty of the Advocate will increase his reputations and respect in the society.
2. ***Industry:*** It means hard work. Hard works is absolutely necessary for an Advocate. His knowledge of law should be up to date. He shall never be ignorant of the current law in force. He shall get acquainted with the latest law by systematic study. If one ignores the law, the law will also ignore him. That is why it is said that "law is the jealous mistress".
3. ***Justice:*** An Advocate is as an Officer of the High Court. He should help the Judge in finding out the truth in the dispute, and help him to arrive the right decision. For

this purpose, he shall submit the proper position of the law, facts and evidence related to the case. An Advocate has to protect the interest of the client, but at the same time he must realize that he is not the mere mouth piece of the client. Therefore, he shall never resort to unfair the practices. His efforts should be always to advance the cause of the justice.

4. ***Service:*** Legal profession mainly concerned with the promotion of administration of justice and the establishment of the welfare society. Therefore, Lawyers shall be willing to protect the right of the oppressed and the poor. They shall render their service to the general public without any discrimination.
5. ***Philosophy:*** Lawyers should have some Philosophical outlook. An Advocate has to deal with the variety of disputes both favorable and unfavorable to his client. So, he should have the required mental fitness to adjust and accommodate with the changes. It is therefore necessary that lawyers should be guided by some philosophical principles suitable to the profession.

11

Ten commandments of Advocates

The various duties of an Advocate like duties to the client, duties to the court, duties to the colleagues and duties to the public shall be put into the following ten rules popularly known as the ten Commandments of Advocates.

1. ***Protection of the interest of the client:*** An Advocate must be loyal to the interests of the client and fight for his cause without the fear of any unpleasant consequence to him or any other person (see duty to the client).
2. ***Proper Estimation of the value of the Legal Advice:*** An Advocate shall not over estimate or under estimate the value of his advice. He must always give proper legal advice to the client.
3. ***Honest and Respect:*** He must be always honest and respectful to the court.
4. ***Preparation of the case:*** He must prepare the case thoroughly before presenting it to the court.
5. ***Service:*** Lawyers shall be willing to protect the rights of the oppressed and the poor.

6. ***Loyalty to Law and Justice:*** He must always give advice to enhance loyalty to law and justice.
7. ***Fellowship:*** He must be always friendly with the fellow-members of the Bar and more friendly with the young lawyers and encourage them.
8. ***Fairness:*** He must be fair in his dealings with the client, with the court and with the public
9. ***Systematic Study:*** He must develop the habit of systematic study of the law and acquainted with the latest developments in Law.
10. ***Prudence and Diligence:*** He must always vigilant and active. He must avoid the easy come and easy-go method.

12

Darwin's Theory in Legal Profession.

Darwin's theory is that 'Survival of the Fittest'. It means that only fit person will survive and others cannot survive in this world. This theory very much implies to the legal person also. It is true that only professionally fit person alone can survive in the legal profession and others cannot survive. Though every lawyers are entering the profession, only very few of them continue in the legal profession, and others leave the profession in the middle.

One can survive in the legal profession, only he acquires the good qualities of Advocacy, immediately after joining the profession. If he fails to do so, he will be compelled to leave the profession when others lawyers who possess the qualities of Advocacy are leading in the profession. So, one should keep it in mind and act accordingly to get the good qualities of Advocacy.

13

Meaning of Professional Ethics

The word 'ethics derived from the Greek word 'ethos'. It means the habitual mode of conduct Professional ethics means a conduct written or unwritten which prescribes the duties of a profession (legal Profession).

The legal Profession and the judiciary as a whole in all countries have been honored as the 'pure fountain of justice' and enjoys high esteem of respect. In order to maintain the respect, lawyers have to follow certain ethical regulations.

S.49(I) (C) of the Advocates Act, 1961 empowers the bar council of India to make rules prescribing the standards of professional conduct and etiquette to be observed by the advocates. The rules made by the Bar council shall come into effect only when it is approved by the Chief justice of India.

In exercise of this rule making power the Bar Council of India has made several rules prescribing the standards of professional conduct and etiquette for the advocates. These rules specify the duties of an Advocate to the court, client, opponent and colleagues etc. These rules are broadly called as professional ethics.

Meaning of the term Etiquette

The term etiquette is slightly different from the term ethics. It refers to the pattern of behavior and the mode in which the person is required to conduct himself. It springs from the long habit and custom. Etiquette consists of the following elements namely, elegance, dignity and decency. The legal profession observes these things as an etiquette. In order to protect the dignity of the profession the members must observe the etiquette very strictly. The etiquette requires that an Advocate should behave himself as an officer of the court, a privileged member of the community and a gentleman.

14

Duties of Advocates

In the administration of the justice, the role of the advocate is to help the court to take a right decision in the dispute. While performing this job, an Advocate is duty bound to perform certain duties to the court. Following are duties prescribed by the Bar Council rules as duty to the court, which should be observed by the Advocates.

1. DUTIES TOWARDS COURT

Section 1 of Chapter II of Part VI of the Bar Council of India Rules are the rules related to 'Advocates Duty To the Court'.

1) An advocate should be straightforward and his arguments should be pointed, clear, precise and concise.

2) An advocate should have sense of humor and pleasing manners in his arguments.

3) An advocate must be tactful in presenting the matters.

4)An Advocate should not mislead the Court .

5) An advocate shall not influence the decision of the court by any illegal or improper Means.

6) An advocate shall appear in the court at all times only in the prescribed dress. He shall not wear a band or gown in public places other than in Courts.

7) An advocate shall, when presenting his case and while otherwise acting before a court, conduct himself with dignity and self respect.

8) An Advocate shall not enter appearance, act, plead or practice in any way before a Court , tribunal or authority on behalf of close kith and Kin.

9) An advocate shall not criticize the Judiciary with malice .

10) An advocate should not act or plead in any matter in which he himself pecuniarily interested .

11)An advocate shall not stand as a surety or certify the soundness of a surety for his client, required for the purpose of any legal proceedings.

12) An advocate Shall assist court by presenting fully the pertinent law in his case.

2. DUTIES TOWARDS CLIENTS

Section 2 of Chapter II of Part VI of Bar Council India Rules provides the provisions relating to an advocate's duty to clients.

1) An advocate shall fearlessly uphold the interests of his client by All fair and honorable means without regard any unpleasant consequences to himself or any other .

2) An advocate shall fairly and reasonably submit the case on behalf of his client.

3) An advocate shall pay attention which he is capable of giving to the case he is dealing.

4) An advocate shall not act on the instructions of any person either than his Client or authorised agent.

5)An advocate shall not ordinarily withdraw from engagements ones accepted, without sufficient cause and unless reasonable and sufficient notice is given to the client.

6) An advocate shall not do anything whereby be abuses or takes advantage. of the confidence reposed in him by his client.

7) An advocate shall not accept a fee less than the fee taxable under the rules when the client is able to pay the same .

8) An advocate shall not adjust fee payable to him by his client against his own personal liability to the client which liability does not arise in the course of his employment as an advocate.

9) An advocate should keep accounts of the clients money entrusted to him.

10) An advocate shall not lend money to his client for the purpose of any action or legal proceedings in which he is engaged by such client.

11) An advocate shall not disclose Communications made to them in course of their professional engagement even after the case is over.

3. DUTIES TOWARDS OPPONENT

Section 3 of Chapter II of Part VI of the Bar Council of India Rules provides for the duties of an advocate to the opposing party.

1) An advocate shall not communicate or negotiate upon the subject matter of controversy with any party represented by an advocate except through that advocate.

2) An advocate shall not mislead an opponent, or put him on the wrong scent regarding any point in the case.

3) An Advocate shall do his best to carry out all legitimate promises made to the opposite party even though not reduced to writing.

4. DUTIES TOWARDS COLLEAGUES

Section 4 of Chapter II of Part VI of the Bar Council of India Rules describes the duties of an advocate towards his colleagues.

1) An advocate shall not solicit work or advice directly or indirectly through Mass Communication.

2) An advocate shall not pursue his profession in spirit of competition or rivalry, with his brethren.

3) An advocate should be courteous to opposing Counsel and should accede io reasonable request regarding Court proceedings .

4) An advocate shall not enter appearance in any case in which there is already a vakalatnama or Memo of appearance filed by an advocate engaged for a party expect with his consent.

5) An advocate does not envy another advocate who attains to position and rank and earns well.

6) An younger advocate must be cordial and relationship and pay respect to senior advocates .

7) An advocates shall be ready to give help and advice to brother members.

8) An advocate shall strive at all the levels aid the legal profession in advancing the standard of members of profession

5.DUTY TOWARDS COMMUNITY

1)An advocate shall establish Legal Aid Societies for the purpose of rendering legal assistance to really poor and deserving persons free of any charge .

2) An advocate shall help the people local bodies such as panchayats in villages to function on sound lines, so that the people may discharge their functions in an enlightened and responsible manner.

3) An advocate shall provide Legal education to the illiterate and working people by informing them for the rights and legal provisions in simple language .

4)An advocate shall compose family differences and Settle petty Disputes and controversies by amicable settlement.

5) An advocate shall educate the masses on the right lines to come out of many social ills from which people are suffering.

6) An advocate shall work with social welfare committees to promote social order in which justice ,political ,economic and social will be assured to one .

6. RESTRICTION ON OTHER EMPLOYMENT

An Advocate shall not personally engage in any business but he may be a sleeping partner in a firm doing business provided that, in the opinion of the Bar Council the nature of the business is not inconsistent with the dignity of his legal profession i.e. Advocacy.

An Advocate may be a Director or Chairman of the Board of Directors of a company with or without any ordinary sitting fee, provided none of his duties are of an executive character. He shall not be a Managing Director or a Secretary of any company.

An Advocate shall not be full-time salaried employee of any person, government, firm, corporation etc. as long as he continues to practice and shall, on taking up any such employment, intimate the fact to the Bar Council and shall thereupon cease to practice as an advocate as long as he continues in such employment.

An Advocate who has inherited, or succeeded by survivorship any family business may continue but is not allowed to personally participate in the management. He may continue to hold a share with others in any business which has descended to him by survivorship or inheritance or by will, but he does not personally participate in the management of that business.

An advocate may review Parliamentary Bills for a remuneration, edit legal text books at a salary, do press-vetting for newspapers, coach pupils for legal examination, set and examine question papers.

An advocate can also engage in broadcasting, journalism, lecturing and teaching subjects, both legal and non-legal but this should be in accordance with the other rules about advertising and full-time employment.

7. RESTRICTION TO ADVERTISEMENT

Rule 36 of Bar Council of India restricts the Advocates not to advertise about the profession. This restriction is imposed because Advocate profession is the noble profession.

Due to this restriction Advocates are banned to do the followingthings.

1. Directly or indirectly advertise about their profession.
2. Publishing his photo along the news regarding his appearance in a case.
3. Circulation of pamphlets or giving advertisement with a view of soliciting case.

15

Professional Misconduct

1. MEANING

Misconduct means dereliction of duty. Professional misconduct means dereliction of duty relating to Legal profession. Under S.35 of the Advocates Act, An Advocate is punishable not only for professional misconduct but also for other misconduct. Other misconduct means a misconduct not directly connected with the legal profession.

Professional misconduct arises as a result of serious dereliction of duties to the court, to the client, to the opponent, to the colleagues, to the profession, to the public etc. Following are some of the instances of professional misconduct.

1. Making false allegation against judicial officers.
2. Deliberately lodging groundless criminal complaint.
3. Making groundless and insulting charges against witness.
4. Refusing to accept a case without justification.

5. Attending court proceedings in drunken state.
6. Attempting to influence judicial officers for favor.
7. Carrying on other trade or business.
8. Committing crimes.
9. Financing litigation.
10. Obtaining client's signature on blank papers.
11. Shouting slogans or holding demonstration in front of the court.
12. Approaching investigative officers for favor during investigation of a case.
13. Writing letter to the presiding officer in connection with the pending case.
14. Tampering with the witness
15. Suggesting the client to bribe the presiding officer.
16. Moving application before any court or authority before informing that a similar application has been presented before any authority or rejected by any authority.
17. An exclusively retained pleader accepting a case against the client from the opposite party.
18. Failure to appear in the proceedings of a case without any sufficient reason.
19. Retaining the judgement of the trial court with the intention of getting himself getting himself engaged in appeal.
20. Presenting the plaint with in sufficient court fee stamp, when the client has given money for the court fee.
21. Alleging partiality against presiding officer in open court.
22. Tampering with records and documents.
23. Writing letters to persons for soliciting cases.
24. Reporting no instructions from his client and subsequently appearing for the opposite party in the same suit.

25. Advertising about his profession.
26. Taking advantage of the ignorance and illiteracy of the clients, demanding money from them on false representations that is required for court purposes and misappropriating the same.
27. Misappropriation of decreed amount payable to the client.
28. Giving wrong advise to the client.
29. Taking money from the client for the purpose of giving bribe.
30. Suppression of truth.
31. Changing sides.
32. Indecent cross examination.
33. Committing contempt of court.
34. False identifications of deponents.
35. Gross negligence involving moral turpitude.
36. Appearing without authority i.e. On forged vakalath.
37. Failure to attend the trial.
38. Attesting forged affidavit.
39. Abstaining from appearing in court on the ground of strike called by the Bar association.
40. Misleading the court resulting in erroneous order.

2. PUNISHMENT OF PROFESSIONAL MISCONDUCT

The Disciplinary committee of the State Bar Council after hearing the Advocate concerned and the Advocate general comes to the conclusion that the misconduct is proved that it may pass any of the following orders, namely

i. Reprimand the Advocate.
ii. Suspend the Advocate from the practice for such period as it thinks fit.

iii. Remove the name of the Advocate from the Advocates Roll.

Punishment may be awarded depending on the gravity of misconduct established against him. The punishment to remove from the Advocates Roll is awarded only in the cases where the misconduct is of such nature that the Advocate is unworthy of remaining in the profession.

Where an Advocate is suspended from the practice he shall not practice in any court or tribunal or any authority or person during the suspended period.

Where notice is issued to the Advocate general, he may appear before the disciplinary committee in person or through any Advocate appearing on his behalf. If the misconduct is not proved beyond reasonable doubt, then the disciplinary committee shall dismiss the petition.

3. REMEDIES

Appeal to the Bar council of India (s 37)

Any person aggrieved by the order of the disciplinary committee of the State Bar Council, or the Advocate general of the State may within 60 days from the date of the order may prefer an appeal to the Bar Council of India. The appeal shall be filed in person or through by Advocate or by registered post. He must submit 5 copies of appeal memorandum along with the attested copy of the order of the State Bar Council.

Such appeal shall be heard by the disciplinary committee of the Bar Council of India and after hearing it may pass any order it deems fit i.e., it can confirm. The order of the State Bar Council, or increase or reduce the punishment, or totally remove the punishment.

Appeal to the Supreme Court

Any person aggrieved by an order made by the Disciplinary committee of the Bar Council of India, or the Attorney General of India may within 60 days from the date of order prefer an appeal to the Supreme court. The Supreme Court after hearing the parties concerned shall pass any order as it thinks fit.

Normally, the Supreme court will not interfere with the concurrent findings of fact by the disciplinary committee of the Bar Council of India and the State Bar Council. If the finding is based on no evidence, then the court will examine it.

Stay of the order

For the convenience of filing an appeal against the order of the State Bar Council or the Bar Council of India, the aggrieved party can file an application before the concerned Bar Council which has passed the order to stay the order still appeal is filed. If genuine grounds are there then the concerned Bar Council can stay the order.

Review of its own order by the State Bar Council

According to S.44, the Disciplinary committee of a State Bar council is empowered to review its own order either on its own motion or an application by the aggrieved party within 60 days from the date of order.

In the review proceedings also the State Bar council will hear the concerned parties before making any order.

Any order passed in review by the disciplinary committee of the state Bar Council shall have effect only when it is approved by the Bar Council of India.

The Disciplinary committee of the Bar Council of India has no power to review its own order (S.48 AA).

16

Disciplinary Committee

Disciplinary Committee of the State Bar Council

Organization

S.9 of the Advocates Act empowers the state Bar Councils to constitute one or more Disciplinary Committees. Each Disciplinary Committee shall consist of 3 members. Two shall be selected from the members of the Bar Council and one shall be selected from the Advocates who are having more than 10 years of standing in profession. Among the three members the senior most in the profession shall act as the chairman of the committee.

Powers

S.42 of the Advocates Act deals with the power of Disciplinary committee. It provides that the Disciplinary Committee of the State Bar Council shall have the same powers same like the civil court under the C.P.C. in respect of the following matters.

1. Summoning and enforcing the attendance of any person and examining him on oath.
2. Requiring discovery and production of any documents.
3. Receiving evidence on affidavit.

4. Requiring any public record or copies of any record from any court or office.
5. Issuing commissions for the examinations of witness or documents.

The disciplinary committee has no right to require the attendance of the following persons.

i. Any presiding officer of the court.
ii. Any officer of the revenue court.

A presiding officer of a court shall be summoned to attend the proceedings of the Disciplinary Committee with permission of the High Court and an officer of the revenue court shall be summoned with the permission of the State Govt.

All the proceedings before the Disciplinary Committee of a Bar Council shall be deemed to a judicial proceeding within the meaning of

S.193 & 228 of I.P.C and every such disciplinary Committee shall be deemed to be a civil court.

Enquiry Procedure

The main function of the Disciplinary Committee of the Bar Council is to enquire the complaints of professional misconduct against the Advocates award suitable punishments. In the enquiry the following procedures prescribe under S.35 of the Advocates Act should be followed.

1. On perusal of the complaint, if the Bar council is satisfied that it is a fit case for enquiry then the complaint shall be referred for enquiry to the Disciplinary Committee.

2. The Disciplinary Committee shall fix a date for enquiry and shall send notice to the concerned Advocate and the Advocate General of the State.
3. The Advocate charged with the professional misconduct shall appear in person or through the Lawyer. Similarly, the Advocate general also appear in person or through a lawyer.
4. The Disciplinary Committee should complete the enquiry proceedings within one year from the date of receipt of the complaint. Due to any reason, if the enquiry was not completed within one year, then the complaint should be referred to the Bar Council of India for its disposal.
5. During the pendency of the enquiry if the term of the Disciplinary Committee comes to an end, then the successor committee shall continue the enquiry.
6. After the enquiry due to the lack of majority opinion or otherwise if the Disciplinary Committee was unable to take a final decision, then they shall seek the opinion of the chairman of the bar council and shall pass the final order following his opinion.

Disciplinary Committee of the Bar Council of India

Powers: The Disciplinary Committee of the Bar Council of India shall have the following powers.

1. It shall enquire the charges of the professional misconduct against Advocates whose name is there in the roll of any of the State Bar Council.
2. Enquire the complaints in which the Disciplinary Committee of the State Bar Council has not completed the enquiry within one year from the date of receipt of

the complaint.

3. Hear the appeal against the order of the State Bar Council.
4. Allowing the State Bar Council to review its own order.

Just like the Disciplinary Committee of the State Bar Council, the Bar Council of India Disciplinary committee is also having powers like a civil court.

Transfer of proceedings from the State Bar Council to the Bar Council of India

If the State Bar Council after verification is satisfied that the charges of professional misconduct are a fit case for enquiry then it shall refer it to the Disciplinary Committee for the enquiry.

The Disciplinary Committee must complete the enquiry proceedings within one year from the date of receipt. The main object of putting a time bound enquiry is speedy disposal of the cases. Due to any reason, if the enquiry was not completed within a year, then the complaint should be transferred to the Bar Council of India for enquiry. The transfer should be made by the Suo-moto by the State Bar Council (S.36 B).

The complaints so transferred shall be enquired by the Disciplinary Committee of the Bar Council of India and pass suitable orders as it thinks fit. There is no time limit for the Bar Council of India to complete the enquiry.

The **Supreme Court** stated in the case of State of Punjab v. Ram Singh Ex. Constable that "misconduct in office" is defined as "unlawful behaviour or neglect by a public officer that affects a party's rights." In addition, the court noted that professional misconduct could include:

a. Moral Turpitude.

b. Wrongful or improper behaviour

c. Wilful and unlawful behaviour is a prohibited act

d. encroachment

e. The act complained of bears a forbidden quality or character due to carelessness or negligence in the performance of duty.

The term "Professional Misconduct" is not defined anywhere in the Advocates Act, and a standard definition is impossible to come up with. As a result, precedents in this area are the only reliable source of information about what constitutes professional misconduct.

17

Important Cases On Professional Misconduct

Shambhu Ram Yadav vs Hanum Das Khatry AIR 2001SC 2509

In the case, the respondent wrote a letter to his client and asked him to bribe the judge so that he could help the client win the case. The respondent was held guilty here of misconduct under Section 35 of the Advocates Act, for bribing a Judge and the State Bar Council suspended him from practice for a period of two years. The respondent challenged the aforesaid order before the Disciplinary Committee of the Bar Council of India, by order dated 31st July 1999, the Disciplinary Committee of the Bar Council of India comprising of three members enhanced the punishment and directed that the name of the respondent be struck off from the roll of advocates, thus debarring him permanently from the practice. The respondent further moved to the Honourable Supreme Court of India. The

Honourable Supreme Court here upheld the decision of the Disciplinary Committee of the Bar Council of India, and also mentioned that "Legal profession is not a trade or business. It is a noble profession".

P.D. Gupta v.Ram Murthi (AIR 1998 SC 283)

One Mr. Krishnan died on 5-6-1980. His sister Vidyawati filed a suit for decleration of title in her favour for certain properties of Mr. Krishnan, Ram Murthi and others resisted the suit claiming title in their favour. P.D.Gupta was the Advocate of Vidyawati. When the suit was pending P.D. Gupta purchased part of the disputed property for Rs.18000 and sold it for 34000 immediately.

Mr. Ram Murthi filed a complaint against P.D.Gupta before the Delhi Bar Council alleging professional misconduct. The main allegation is that he has purchased the part of the disputed property from his client during the pendency of the suit. Since the enquiry was not completed within one year the matter is transferred to the Bar Council of India. After hearing both the parties, the Bar Council of India passed an order suspending him from the practice for a period of one year. The court held that a shadow of undue influence is present when an Advocate buys property of his own client.

Against this order P.D. Gupta filed an appeal before the Supreme court. In the appeal his main contention was that his client or her legal heirs has not filed any complaint regarding professional misconduct, and the enquiry conducted based on the complaint by some other person is wrong. The Supreme Court did not accept this argument and passed the following orders.

1. Any person shall file a complaint regarding professional misconduct against an Advocate.

2. Bar council shall enquire into the allegation of professional misconduct, though the complaint is filed by a stranger, because, the Bar council is concerned with the conduct of Advocates.
3. The order passed by the Bar Council of India is confirmed.

Prahalad Saran Gupta v. Bar Council of India (AIR 1997 Sc 1338)

Gupta was practicing Advocate at Ghaziabad . He was appearing for the decree-hold in an execution case between Atma Ram manak Chand v. Shriram in the Ghaziabad court. The degree holder has filed a complaint in the State Bar Council against his Advocate (Gupta) alleging the following professional misconduct.

1. He has colluded with the judgement debtor and accepted Rs. 1500 out of the total decreed amount and allowed time for the payment of the remaining balance.
2. The amount so received is not given to the degree holder.
3. He has helped the judgement Debtor to get the execution stayed by the High Court.
4. When he was Acting as a standing counsel for the railways, he drafted the notice under S.80.C.P.C to be served to the railways on behalf of M/s. Agarwal traders who was the compliment against the Railways. This is a serious professional misconduct. The draft prepared by his own handwriting was produced before the disciplinary committee.

Gupta denied all the allegations and informed that he was holding the amount of Rs.1500 as trustee on behalf of his client. Since the enquiry was not completed within one year the matter was transferred to the Bar Council of India.

The Bar council of India has found the appellant guilty of serious professional misconduct and passed an order suspending him from the practice for a period of one year. Gupta challenged this order before the Supreme court. The Supreme court passed the following orders.

1. It is not advisable for the Disciplinary Committee to base its conclusion purely on the basis of its own comparison of the hand writing of Gupta with the alleged draft prepared by him. The court held that the charge of professional misconduct is quasi- criminal in nature requires proof beyond reasonable doubt.
2. Addressing a letter to the counsel of the opposite party (judgement debtor) in the execution proceedings amounts to professional misconduct.
3. Holding the money with him which he has received in the execution proceedings without any sufficient reason amounts to professional misconduct.
4. For this misconduct suspending him from practice for 1 year is too much, So the Bar Council of India's order is set aside and he was reprimanded with strong words.

Banu Murthy v. Bar Council of Andhra Pradesh DC Appeal No.3/1994

The appellant was a member of the Andhra Pradesh Judicial service. When he was working as Metropolitan Magistrate at Hyderabad there were certain allegations of corruption against him. A departmental enquiry was conducted and e was served with an order of compulsory retirement and retired on 30-7-1991.

After compulsory retirement he applied for resumption of practice. The State Bar Council referred the matter to the Bar Council of India because he had been found guilty by the departmental enquiry. The Bar Council of India returned the matter to the Disciplinary Committee of the State Bar Council found him guilty of professional misconduct and suspended him from practice for a period of 2 years. Against this order the present appeal has been filed.

When the appeal was pending, he was allowed to resume his practice from 6-4-1994 by some court order. Bar Council of India continued the enquiry and finally held that since 2 years has already lapsed since his punishment for corruption charges, he shall resume his practice.

Hikmat Ali khan v. Ishwar Prasad Arya (AIR 1977 SC 864)

Ishwar Prasad Arya was an Advocate practicing in Badann, U.P. He stabbed his opponent with the knife for that he has convicted 3 years rigorous imprisonment. On appeal the High court also confirmed the punishment.

Thereafter, by using a forged letter of the Governor asking the court to suspend his sentence under art. 161 of the constitution he got his conviction suspended and he was released. Later the sessions Judge found the letter as forged one and he lodged a complaint with the Bar Council of U.P. for necessary action against him. The State Bar Council debarred him from practice for 2 years. On appeal the Bar Council of India set aside this order on the ground that there is no clear evidence to show that the Advocate himself has prepared that forged letter.

Subsequently by taking into account of the bad conduct of the Advocate i.e., Conviction for the offence under S.307 of I.P.C and his name being entered by the police in a register which contains the list of persons with bad character he was debarred for the practice for a period of

3 years by the State Bar Council. On appeal this order was also set aside by the Bar Council of India because it is interconnected with the earlier matter. Hikmit Ali Khan preferred an appeal before Supreme Court against this order.

The Supreme court held that the second order of the State Bar Council was based on totally a different ground not connected with the grounds of the first order and the Bar Council of India was erroneous in setting aside the second order of the U.P. Bar Council. Further Supreme court held that the gravity of the misconduct committed by him is so serious and the punishment of suspending him from practice for 3 years is not sufficient and ordered the removal of his name from the roll of Advocates.

Smt. Sudesh Rani v. Munish Chandra Goel (2002) 1 UPLBEC 654

The respondent advocate filed suits for the eviction of the tenants by suppressing the fact that an earlier compromise decree was passed wherein the tenants were declared as owners of the said property. The respondent advocate suppressed the material facts since his wife and he were involved in the compromise of the suits. The advocate was found guilty of misconduct and suspended for two years.

Suo Moto Enquiry v. Nand Lal Balwani (1999) 2 SCC 743

The Respondent Advocate hurled shoes and shouted slogans in the Supreme Court of India, which lead to both contempt and misconduct proceedings against him. The Supreme Court found him to be guilty of contempt and the BCI found him guilty of misconduct and removed him from the roll.

Prof. Krishanraj v. Vishwanth D. Mukashikar, BCI Tr. Case No. 49/1999

In this case, the fact are the Advocate in disgrace had made delay in filing the suit and even the interim application causing consequent loss to the client, held him guilty of misconduct.

Noratanmal Chaurasia v. M.R. Murli AIR 2004 SC 2440

The supreme court held that "misconduct is not defined under the Advocates Act, 1966 but misconduct envisages breach of discipline, although it would not be possible to lay down exhaustively as to what would constitute misconduct and indiscipline which, however, is wide enough to include wrongful omission or commission, whether done or omitted to be done intentionally or unintentionally"

18

Contempt of Court

CONTEMPT OF COURT

Object of the Act

The main object of the contempt of court Act is to protect the dignity and decorum of the court and to uphold the majesty of law. The object is not to protect the judges from criticism. By providing punishment for contempt of the court the ability to deliver fearless and impartial justice is strengthened.

Definition

The definition given in the Act for the term contempt of court is not exhaustive. it is difficult to define it by words, because the scope of contempt of court is very wide. Contempt means

i. Any disrespect to the authority of law.
ii. Disobedience of the order of the court.
iii. Disturbance to the proceedings of the court.

Types

Following are the types of contempt (i) Civil contempt and(ii)Criminal contempt.

CIVIL CONTEMPT

S.2(b)defines the term `civil contempt'. 'It means (i)Willful disobedience to any judgement, decree, direction, order, writ or other process of a court; or(ii)Willful breach of an undertaking given to a court.

For taking action for civil contempt on the ground of willful disobedience of court order, it should be established that the court which has passed the order has jurisdiction to pass such order. Disobedience of an order passed without jurisdiction is not a Contempt must prove that the court has no jurisdiction.

A willful breach of an unconditional undertaking given orally or in writing either in person or through his Advocate will be treated as civil contempt. When undertakings are given orally, the court shall record it in the proceedings.

Breach of a compromise entered in the court cannot be treated as civil contempt. The remedy in such cases is only a civil suit for specific performance of the promise.

Punishment

S.12 prescribes the punishment for contempt court may award any one of the following punishments.

i. Simple imprisonment for a term which may extend to 6 months.
ii. Fine which may extend to Rs.2000/-
iii. Both the punishment i.e., Imprisonment and fine together.

CRIMINAL CONTEMPT

S.2(c)defines the term `criminal contempt'. It means

i. Publication of any matter (by words, spoken or written, or by signs or by visible representation or otherwise.)

ii. Doing of any other act which

a. Scandalizes or Tenda to scandalize, or lowers or tends to lower the authority of any court; or
b. Prejudices or interferes or tends to interfere with the due course of judicial proceeding; or
c. Interferes or tends to interfere with, or obstructs or tends to obstruct the Administration of justice.

Publication means publishing something orally or in writing through newspaper, pamphlets, radio, television or cinema. conversation between two persons cannot be treated as publication.

To decide criminal contempt, the absence of criminal intention on the part of the person who has published the matter containing criminal contempt or done the act of contempt will not be taken into account.

In ***E.M.S. Nambothribad v. T.N. Mambiar*** (AIR 1970 SC 2015) the then Chief Minister of Kerala, Mr. Nambothribad in a press meet expressed the following about judiciary, judiciary is responsible for the suppression of people. Judges are favoring some class of people and working against the other classes. Judiciary is acting against the interest of working class and the agriculturist. judiciary is helping the oppressor group. The supreme court held that the act of Mr. Nambothribad amounts to criminal contempt.

Punishment

S.12 prescribes the punishment for contempt court may award any one of the following punishments.

1.Simple imprisonment for a term which may extend to 6 months.

2.Fine which may extend to Rs.2000/-.

3.Both the punishments i.e., imprisonment and fine together.

Delhi Judicial Services Association v. State of Gujarat (AIR 1991 SC 2176) the Supreme Court held punishment not mentioned in S.12 can also be given for contempt of court.

In R***e Vinay Chandra Mishra*** (AIR 1995 SC2348) the supreme court held that for contempt of court committed by an Advocate, he shall be suspended from practice for a fixed period or he shall be permanently restrained from practice. The Supreme Court Bar Association has filed a review petition against this order. In which the supreme court held that for contempt of court the court cannot cancel the Advocates right to practice. But he shall be suspended from practice for a fixed period.

For the civil contempt, normally fine alone will be imposed. If the court thinks that fine alone is not a sufficient punishment then he shall be put in the civil prison instead of ordinary imprisonment.

If the contempt of court is committed by a company in collusion of the Directors, Secretary and other Managerial staff then shall be detained in the civil prison.

If the contempt is committed by a firm, then the punishment shall be enforced against the partners of the firm.

DEFENCES OF CONTEMPT

A. DEFENCES FOR CRIMINAL COMTEMPT

S.3 to 7 deals with the defences available in Criminal Contempt. They are as follows:

1. ***Innocent Publication (S.3):*** A person shall not be guilty of contempt of court if he had made any innocent publication of any matter pending before a court

without knowing that the matter is pending a court. The person charge with contempt must prove that publication is made without knowing that the Matter is pending in the court.

2. ***Publication Relating to a Decided Case (S.3(2)):*** Publication about the decided case is not a contempt since the case is already decided by the court, the publication is not going to interfere with the disposal of the case. that is why it is not treated as contempt.
3. ***Distribution of publication without knowing that it contains contempt of court Matter (S.3(3)):*** If a person distributes and publication without knowing that it contains contempt of court matter then it cannot be treated as contempt. If the publication does not contain the name and address of the Author, publisher and printer then this defence cannot be used by the person distributing such publications.
4. ***Fair and Accurate Reporting of Judicial Proceedings (S.4):*** Fair and accurate reporting of judicial proceedings is not a contempt. This is because we are following the principle of openness in the matter of administration of justice.

The following reporting of judicial proceedings though it is fair and accurate it will be treated as contempt of court.

a. Reporting of the proceedings against any law which is in force.

b. Reporting of the proceedings when the court has prohibited the reporting in the interest of the general public.

c. Reporting of the proceedings conducted in the judges' chamber in the interest of defence of public order.

d. Reporting of information relating to secret process, discovery or invention which is an issue in the case.

5. Fair Criticism of Judicial Act (S.5): A proper and fair comment on a decision is not a contempt of court. Criticism is permitted to the extent where it does not interfere with the administration of justice. So, it is open to anyone to express fair, reasonable and legitimate criticism of a judicial decision.

6. Bonafide Complaint against the Presiding Officers of a subordinate court (S.6): A bonafide complaint made in good faith against the presiding officer of a subordinate court to the higher authorities, who have control over such subordinate court, is not a contempt.

No Substantial Interference with the Administration of Justice: It means an act which is technically a contempt but such act does snot substantially interfere with the administration of justice. For such acts no punishment is awarded.

B. DEFENCES FOR CIVIL COMTEMPT

Following are some of the important defences available to a person charged with civil contempt.

1. **Disobedience of the Order is Not Willful:** If the disobedience of the order is accidental or which is not willful then it's a good defence in a civil contempt proceeding.
2. **The Order Passed Without Jurisdiction:** If the order passed by the court is without jurisdiction, then the disobedience or violation of such order cannot be treated as contempt of court. An order passed without jurisdiction is void, hence it won't bind any person. The person charged with contempt must prove that the court has no jurisdiction to pass such

order.

3. **Order Disobeyed is Vague or Ambiguous:** An order is treated as vague if it is not clear, specific and complete. For violation of such order contempt proceedings cannot be taken.
4. **Order Involves More than One Reasonable Interpretation:** If the order of the court involves more than reasonable interpretation, and one interpretation is adopted by the party and acted in accordance with such interpretation then he cannot be held liable for contempt of court for not following the order interpretation.
5. **Compliance with the Order is Impossible:** Impossibility means that the implementation of the order is practically not possible

In **Amar Singh v. K.P Geetha Krishnan** (1993, I SCR 465) the court has passed on order to give some benefits to the retired employees. This order was not implemented. In the contempt proceeding it was argued that the implementation of the order involves huge expenditure hence compliance with the order is impossible. The court has not accepted this defence.

6. ***No Knowledge of the Order:*** A person cannot be held liable for civil contempt, if he has no knowledge about the order. If he has knowledge about the order, through it is not officially communicated to him, then he cannot put this defense for violation of the order.

Contempt against Subordinate Court

The Contempt of court Act, 1971 confers power only to the Supreme Court and High Courts to try the contempt of court and award suitable punishment.

Contempt of court against the subordinate courts shall be tried by the High court. The concerned subordinate court or the Advocate General of the state shall file the petition before the High court. In the Union Territories, the officer authorized in this behalf shall file the petition.

A contempt which comes within the definition of S.228 of I.P.C. shall be tried and punished by the subordinate courts.

S.228: When judicial proceedings are going on, a person causing disturbance to the proceedings and thereby shows disrespect to the court shall be punished with simple imprisonment for a term which may extend to 6 months or with a fine which may extend to Rs.1000/-or with both.

In the trial of such cases the court shall follow the procedure laid down in S.345 & 346 of Criminal procedure Code. This section deals with summary procedure. So, the court shall follow summary procedure and no detailed enquiry is needed.

Contempt Procedure in the Supreme Court or the High Court

The Contempt of the court Act confers the following two types of powers to the supreme court and the High courts with regard to contempt of court.

1. Power to punish a person who has committed contempt of court inside the court (S.14).
2. Power to punish a person who has committed contempt of court outside the court (S.15).

1. **Contempt of Court Inside the Court:** When judicial proceedings are going on, if it appears to the court that a person is guilty of contempt of court in their presence then the court shall take the following actions.

i. Pass an order to arrest the person.
ii. Give a notice in writing immediately regarding the charges against him.
iii. Offered him opportunity to make his defense to the charge.
iv. Take such evidence as may be necessary or as may be offered by such person and hear him.

During the trial, if the person charged with contempt applies either orally or in writing, for a trial by some other judge other than the judge in whose presence the alleged contempt is committed then the request along with the statement of facts of the alleged contempt shall be placed before the Chief Justice shall be taken as evidence.

If the case is transferred to some other Judge, then the judge in whose presence the alleged contempt was committed need not appear as witness. The facts submitted by him to the Chief Justice shall be taken as evidence.

During the pendency of the proceedings, the person charged with contempt shall be detained in such custody as the court may specify. He may be released on bail with or without sureties or on a self-bond as the court thinks fit.

In **Sugdev Singh v. Deeja Singh** (AIR 1954 SC 186) the supreme court has advised that to the extent possible, the judge in whose presence the alleged contempt was committed, must avoid to conduct the trial by himself.

2. ***Contempt of Court Outside the Court:*** The supreme court or the High Court shall take action for contempt of court committed outside the court in the following situations.

i. On its own motion.
ii. On a petition made by the Advocate General (in relation to the High Court) (or the Attorney General or the solicitor General) (in relation to the Supreme Court).
iii. On a petition by any other person (if consent is given in writing to file such petition by the Advocate General or Attorney General or Solicitor General as the case may be).

A person cannot file a contempt of court petition without the consent of the Advocate General or the Attorney General or the Solicitor General. After Admitting a petition, the court shall follow the following procedure.

1. Notice shall be sent to the person charged with contempt.
2. Person charged with contempt shall be allowed to submit his defense in an affidavit.
3. The trial shall be conducted by perusing the defenses submitted by him or taking such other evidences as may be necessary.
4. The trial shall be conducted by a bench consisting of two judges.
5. If the court feels that the person charged with contempt may abscond then his properties shall be attached.

Limitation: The limitation period for filing a petition for contempt of court is one year. After one year even the court cannot take action on its own motion (s.20).

Contempt by Judicial Officers

S.16 of the Act deals with contempt by judges, Magistrates and other persons acting Judicially. According to this section these persons are also liable for contempt of his own court or any other court just like an ordinary individual. If they are not made liable for contempt then people may lose faith on judiciary by the contempt act of judges.

Observation or remark made by a Judge regarding a subordinate court in an appeal or revision pending before him shall not be treated as contempt of court.

In ***State of Rajasthan Prakash Chand*** (AIR 1988 SC 1344) the Supreme Court held that S.16 has no application against the judges of the High Court and the Supreme Court. So, they cannot be punished for contempt of court.

In ***B.K. Mishra v. Bhimsen Dixit*** (1973, 1 SCC 446) the Supreme Court held that refusal to follow the decision of the High Court or the Supreme Court by a subordinate court amount to contempt of court.

No Special Privilege for Advocates

In the contempt of court Act, there is no special privilege for Advocates. A contempt of court Act, A contempt of court committed by an Advocate will be dealt with just like a contempt committed by any other person.

19

Important Cases on Contempt of Court

In Re: Prashant Bhushan and another

In Re: Prashant Bhushan and another (2020), was one such landmark case that brought the limelight to the scope of contempt of court. As far as the facts of the case are concerned, Prashant Bhushan, who was known for his exemplary contribution to the legal fraternity tweeted two comments on the administration of justice by the courts and on CJI SA Bobde. Firstly, on 27 June 2020, he posted a tweet that attributed responsibility to the Supreme Court in 'destructing' India's democracy for the past six years. The second tweet was posted on 29 June 2020 that negatively pictured the then Chief Justice of India SA Bobde while riding a motorcycle. Although with regards to the second tweet a petition was filed in the Court, the Supreme Court took suo moto cognizance of the petition and initiated contempt proceedings against Prashant Bhushan on 21 July 2020.

The Court held the prima facie view that the said tweets brought the administration of justice in disrepute and were capable of undermining the dignity and authority of the Supreme Court in general and of CJI's office in particular, in the eyes of the public at large. Thereby, the Court allowed the suo moto contempt proceedings against him.

Prashant Bhushan put forward several contentions before the Hon'ble Court. Some of them being:

Firstly, he argued that the first petition considered by the Supreme Court in the present case was not sanctioned by the Attorney General of India K.K. Venugopalan even though it was essential under Section 15 of the Contempt of Courts Act and Rule 3(c) of the Rules to Regulate Proceedings for Contempt of the Supreme Court, 1975.

Secondly, as far as the tweet of 29 July was concerned, he highlighted that it was his anguishment for the working of the non-physical courts which lead to undermining the fundamental rights of the citizens of the country. He stated that mere accentuating the incongruity of the present situation cannot be called contempt of court. It would otherwise be against the Right to free speech as enshrined under Article 19(1)(a) of the Constitution.

Regarding the 27 July tweet, it was contended that the statement was a bona fide opinion of the contemnor and cannot amount to contempt of court no matter how unpalatable it was to some people.

The Court was of the view that the inherent power of the Supreme Court to take suo moto contempt proceedings without the sanction of the Attorney General was clearly specified in Section 15 of the Contempt of Courts Act and the subsequent Rule 3. Moving further with regards to the tweets, the Court observed that any publication that attacks an individual judge or the court as a whole, casting unwarranted and defamatory perceptions over the character of the judges would be included within the meaning of scandalizing the court. Such an act instils a sense of distrust among the people and impairs their confidence.

The Court observed that defamatory actions against the judges can be viewed as against the judges acting as judges or as individuals. While the latter is not accountable for contempt proceedings, the former is liable to undergo contempt proceedings as it is scandalising the Court itself. If the vilification is directly scandalising the administration of justice, thereby, dwindling the trust and confidence of the public at large, that forms the foundation of justice, towards the judiciary, then such act should mandatorily be punished through contempt proceedings. At last, the Court held that neither the tweets imposed fair criticism on the working of the judiciary nor any bona fide intention was seen behind these tweets. Therefore, the Court held Prashant Bhushan guilty of criminal contempt and a fine of Rupee 1 to be paid by him, in failure of which he would be punished with 3 months imprisonment and be debarred from practicing law for 3 years.

In Re: Hon'ble Justice Shri C.S. Karnan

The case of In Re: Hon'ble Justice Shri C.S. Karnan (2017) was a contempt proceeding against Justice C.S. Karnan who was surrounded by numerous controversies. The facts of the case were Justice Karnan, who was infamous for his actions committed in a courtroom, accused many high court judges of being corrupt, impartial and dependant. A notice was sent to Prime Minister Narendra Modi to take serious actions against his fellow judges. Further, Justice Karnan accused the then Chief Justice of Madras High Court who went against one of his decisions. Justice Karnan also accused the judges of caste-based discrimination against him. He repetitively filed several suo moto cases against his fellow judges who voted for his transfer even after the Supreme Court restrained him from handling any administrative or judicial work.

The Court observed that Justice C.S. Karnan has consistently committed criminal contempt. Justice Karnan has scandalized several judges and accused them of corruption and impartiality without providing any evidence regarding the same. The obnoxious allegations made by him in front of the media and the public at large tarnished the image of the courts and the beliefs of people in the concept of justice. The conduct of the contemnor was both scandalising the court as well as interfering with the court's proceedings. The Court was seemingly shocked at the behaviour of Justice Karnan and stated that his actions constituted the grossest and gravest actions of contempt of court. The Court held him guilty for criminal contempt of court and sentenced him to 6 months imprisonment.

However, the case suffered several atrocities as the procedure followed by the Court was not proper. The Supreme Court formed a 7 judges bench for the case that is generally instituted in exceptional cases. Further, the written apology given by Justice Karnan was ignored by the Court. The Court failed to formulate any substantial issue underlying the case. The decision was also taken in a hush as no amicus curiae was appointed in the case which was an important step and should be observed by the Court.

In Re: Vijay Kurle and others

In Re: Vijay Kurle (2020), Vijay Kurle along with Rashid Khan Pathan and Nilesh Ojha sent two letters dated 20.03.2019 and 19.03.2019 to the Chief Justice of India Ranjan Gogoi. The above letters levelled scandalous allegations against Justice RF Nariman and Justice Vineet Saran.

The Court observed that the said letters showcase highly scurrilous and scandalous allegations against the judges and such allegations cannot be made against judges and the courts. Further, the Court stated that not even an iota of remorse was shown or apology forwarded by the contemnors. This behaviour, therefore, should not be entertained and it should not be let off leniently. The Court also observed that to comment or criticize the court's judgment, people should also first have the knowledge to challenge the integrity and authority of a judge. Therefore, the Court held them guilty of contempt of court and sentenced all the three advocates to undergo simple imprisonment of three months along with a fine of Rs. 2000.

M.V. Jayarajan v. High Court of Kerala

In the case of M.V. Jayarajan v. High Court of Kerala (2015), the appellant, while delivering a speech at a public gathering at Kannur in June 2010, used unparliamentary words and abused the Kerala High Courts judgment banning meetings on public roads. Considering the pejorative language used by the appellant, the Kerala High Court initiated contempt proceedings against him and later upheld him guilty of contempt of court and sentenced him to imprisonment for a period of six months. To this order, the appellant filed an appeal in the Apex Court.

The Court observed that any foul language used against the court or disrupting the administration of justice should be combated and prevented. Any encumbrance faced by the judiciary in tendering any judgment is said to obstruct the dispensing of justice and must be repulsed. The Court stated that no person can use abusive language against the judges and threaten them to step down from their offices. Further, the Court observed that the appellant showed no remorse or guilt and was not apologetic for his remarks against the judges. Therefore, the Court upheld the decision of the Kerala High Court except it reduced the sentence from six months to four months.

Hari Singh Nagra v. Kapil Sibal

In the case of Hari Singh Nagra and others Vs Kapil Sibal and others (2010), the concept of fair and reasonable criticism was established with respect to contempt proceedings. Referring to the facts of the case, advocate Kapil Sibal along with others sent a souvenir to be published by an association of lawyers while expressing his concern about the plight of the junior members of the Bar and the falling standards of the legal fraternity. Initially, the souvenir was neither published in the public domain nor was made available for sale, rather it was distributed only among the members of the Bar. However, when the respondent was contesting the elections for the Supreme Court Bar Association, certain excerpts of his souvenir were published in the Times of India newspaper. It was then claimed by the petitioners that the said souvenir was deliberated to bring disrepute to the administration of justice and the functioning of the courts.

The Court has stepped beyond the narrow confines of the contempt proceedings and established the concept of "fair" criticism. The Court observed that any ridicule brought towards the judges and the courts, that hampers the confidence and belief of the public thereby deteriorating the foundation of justice must be prevented at all times. But any criticism which is reasonable, rational and sober, not coloured by any tactics must be welcomed. In accordance with Article 19(1)(a) of the Constitution, freedom of speech and expression when used by the Press and the people to fairly criticize any judgment of the court, then no criminal contempt is said to be committed in such cases. Rather it is treated as a necessary right of the people. Therefore, fair and reasonable criticism on the working of the judges and the courts can be made without condemning it as contempt of court.

Abhyudaya Mishra v. Kunal Kamra

The case of Abhyudaya Mishra v. Kunal Kamra was initiated in the year 2020 and is still under trial. But, the case has brought the concept of contempt of court into the limelight. The famous stand-up comedian Kunal Kamra has been alleged to have scandalised the court by degrading its authority through the publication of tweets on social media. The said tweets criticised the Supreme Court for the way it fast-tracked the bail plea of Arnab Goswami, the Chief of Republic TV, in abetment to a suicide case. Attorney General KK Venugopalan gave his assent to initiate the contempt proceedings against Kamra stating that his tweets were of bad taste and that it was time for people to understand attacking the Supreme Court brazenly would attract punishment. In January 2021, the respondent claimed that the jokes are not reality and do not claim to be so and the fact that mere claims can shake the foundation of the Supreme Court will be an overestimation. To this reply of the respondent some rejoinders were requested to which the court gave assent.

Aditya Kashyap v. Rachita Taneja

In yet another ongoing case of Aditya Kashyap v. Rachita Taneja (2020), Rachita Taneja who is a cartoonist was accused of tweeting objectionable content against the court by way of cartoons. The said post went viral and was widely shared and subscribed to. The Attorney General added that such posts are made to degrade the authority of the Supreme Court in the eyes of the public and therefore, even the cartoons were in contempt of the top court. It was contended by the contemnor that fair criticism cannot be upheld to be contempt and that the foundation of the Court is much stronger as one imagines.

Dr. D.C. Saxena v. Hon'ble chief justice of India(AIR 1996 SC 2481)

Dr. D.C. Saxena was a professor of English University. He filed a writ petition in the Supreme Court by way of public interest litigation seeking to recover from the Prime Minister Mr. P.V. Narasima Rao the expenditure incurred for his private use of Indian Air Force Air Craft and Helicopters. The writ petition was dismissed summarily without going into the merits by the bench consisting of Hon'ble chief Justice Mr. A.M Ahmed and others.

Thereafter, Dr. D.C. Saxena filed a second writ petition against the chief justice of India. In this petition he contended that his first writ petition was dismissed by Chief Justice by receiving brief and he prayed for the following.

1. The respondent be declared as unfit to hold the office of chief justice of India.
2. His citizenship should be withdrawn and a case be registered against him for forgery and fraud.
3. Direction to prosecute the Respondent under the prevention of Corruption Act.
4. Direction to the Chief Justice of India to give from his pocket the expenses incurred for filling this writ petition.

The Supreme court issued a show cause notice against him for contempt of court because several averments in the writ petition are scandalous, and the allegation made are reckless attack on the chief justice of India.

Saxena denied all the allegations. He pleaded that he had filed this petition only on public interest and there is no bad intention in filing this petition. He even pleaded that if the court wants, he is ready to withdraw the petition or ready to make the necessary changes in the petition.

The court did not accept this argument and held that withdrawal or making changes in the petition cannot cure the contempt already committed by the scandalous remarks made in the petition. The court passed an order of three months simple imprisonment and a fine of Rs.2000 for contempt of court and the writ petition was also dismissed.

Supreme court Bar Association v. union of India (AIR 1998 SC 1995)

V.C.Mishra, then the Chair Man of the Bar Council of India was punished by the Supreme court for contempt of court and he was suspended from the practice for a period of 3 years. The charges against him were that in the court by using insulting, disrespectful and threatening language he has threatened the judges. His act has hurt the judges and he has acted in such way to abstract the course of justice.

The Supreme Court Bar association challenged this order and raised the following issues.

1. The Supreme Court while dealing with the contempt proceedings cannot suspend Advocate from the practice.
2. Bar Council alone can pass the order suspending an Advocate from practice.
3. For professional misconduct original jurisdiction is vested with the Bar Council.
4. Supreme court vested with only appellate jurisdiction to hear the appeal against the order of the Bar Council of India.

5. Art. 129 of the constitution does not confer any original Jurisdiction to the Supreme court in the matters of professional misconduct.

The main question before the court was whether for contempt of court committed by an Advocate the Supreme Court can pass an order suspending his practice for a specified period.

The Constitution bench of the Supreme Court allowed the petition and issued the following orders.

1. Supreme court's power to punish for contempt is quite wide, yet it is limited.
2. In the contempt of the court proceedings, the court cannot simultaneously enquire into the professional misconduct also by adopting summery procedure.
3. Professional misconduct should be enquired only by following the prescribed procedure mentioned in the Advocates Act.
4. Supreme court can award punishment only for contempt of court and not for professional misconduct.
5. For the contempt of the court, simple imprisonment of 6 weeks is given.
6. This punishment is suspended for 4 years.
7. The punishment shall be activated, if V.C. Mishra again indulges in any other act of contempt of court within the said period of 4 years.

20

Bar Bench Relation

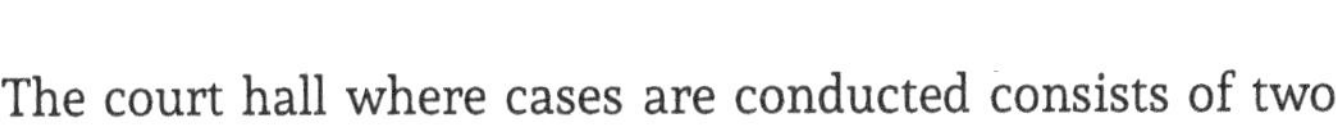

The court hall where cases are conducted consists of two parts namely:

i. The place where the judges sit is called as Bench
ii. The place where the Advocate sit is called as Bar.

So, the term `Bench' refers to the judges and the `Bar' refers to the Advocates. Bar-Bench relation means the cardinal relation between the judges and the Advocates.

The faith on the judiciary to the general public and the speedy justice mainly depends on the cardinal relation between the judges and the Advocates. In the Administration of justice, the role of Advocates is also equally important just like the judges. Rendering justice is their joint responsibility. Without the help of Advocates, it is very difficult for the judges to arrive a correct decision in a dispute.

If good relation exists between exists between the judges and Advocates then delay in rendering justice and high expenses for getting justice can be very much reduced. To strengthen the good relation both should have some good qualities and mutual responsibilities.

Role of the Bar to Strengthen Bar-Bench Relation

To strengthen the Bar-Bench relation, the Advocates must take the following steps.

1. They should give the due respect to the judges and they must avoid speaking ill of the judges and the judiciary.
2. They should help the judges in the trial of the cases by presenting the relevant law in the correct and clear manner. They should never act in such a way to irritate the judges.
3. If the judges pronounce a wrong order, they should not criticize the judges. They should try to set right the wrong order through appeal.
4. For getting favorable order they should not give pressure or influence the judges.
5. If the judge's behavior is irritating and disrespect to the Advocates should not enter in to a direct confrontation with the judge. Through the Bar Association the matter should be discussed with the judge in his chamber and shall request to avoid such misbehavior.
6. Role of the Bench to Strengthen Bar –Bench Relation

Only when Bar-Bench relations are strengthened, people will get confidence and fair on the Judiciary.

To strengthen Bar-Bench relation the Judges should follow and practice the following.

1. ***Judicial Respect:*** Just like the Advocates are giving respect to the Judges the Judges should also give to the Advocates and the brethren Judges.

2. ***Patient Hearing:*** Judges should hear the case with open and respective mind without any prejudice or bias. They should act only to the interest of justice. They should give sufficient opportunity for the Advocates to present the case in full.
3. ***Impartiality:*** Judges should act impartially. They should not act in favor of any Advocate or a party to the dispute.
4. ***Avoidance of Interruptions:*** As far as possible, Judges must avoid interruptions while the Advocate is examining witnesses and arguing the case. Unwarranted interference and adverse comments by the Judges may upset the Advocates and thereby he may not be able to present the case properly. This may cause the failure of justice. Interference may be limited to the following circumstances(i)to prevent repetition and waste of time(ii)to check the relevancy(iii)to get clarifications (iv)to express courts view on a point and (v)to promote speedy disposal of the case.
5. ***Proper Interpretation:*** During the process of administration of justice, often the courts have to interpret the Act, Rules, Orders and Notifications in order to ascertain the actual meaning of the provisions or to remove the ambiguity or inconsistency. In such cases proper interpretation should be given with the object of rendering complete justice to the parties.
6. ***Avoidance of Unreasonable Adjournments:*** Adjournments are given to afford reasonable opportunity to the parties to present the case. As far as possible cases shall not be adjourned without reasonable and sufficient grounds. Unreasonable adjournment is the main reason for the mounting arrears of cases and it causes hardship to the parties.

7. ***Speedy Disposal:*** `Justice delayed is justice denied', hence cases should be disposed of as quickly as possible. When preference is given for disposal of old cases, care should be given to see that new cases should not get into arrears.
8. ***Avoiding Unwarranted comments:*** Judges should not make any unwarranted comments in the open court about the Advocates lack of knowledge in the law. They should not ask any Advocate to leave the court, without sufficient reasons. Similarly, they should not ask any Advocate not to come to his court hereafter.
9. ***Knowing in Law:*** Judges should possess deep knowledge in law. They should have the ability to apply the proper law to the disputed facts and to take the right decision.
10. ***Independence:*** Judges have the primary responsibility to protect and preserve the independence of judiciary, hence they should not yield to the pressure of the Government.
11. ***Integrity:*** A Judge should be honest and morally upright. He should have personal and intellectual integrity. His character and conduct should be praise worthy. Then only the Advocates and the general public will have confidence on him.
12. ***Industriousness:*** It means regular and systematic hard work and study. A Judge should get acquainted with the latest developments and changes in the law by regular updating of the knowledge.
13. ***Meeting of Judges and Lawyers:*** To strengthen Bar-Bench relation, at regular intervals meeting of judges and the Advocates shall be arranged. In such meetings the respective sides difficulties can be discussed and the differences can be sorted out.

21

Accountancy for Lawyer

PURPOSE OF MAINTAINING ACCOUNTS BY LAWYERS

A business enterprise must keep a systematic record of its daily transaction. It is a legal duty. It helps to know where its stand and adjudge its performance. This systematic recording of transactions is known as accounting. Since legal profession is a trade, lawyers are under duty to maintain systematic accounts relating to the profession.

The basic purpose of accounting is to present a complete financial picture of the Advocates profession. This can be done with the help of two financial statements like (i) Profit and loss account and (ii) Balance sheet showing the assets and liabilities.

It is necessary to maintain proper accounts to calculate the following (i) Annual Income (ii) Income Tax (iii) Professional Tax (iv) Amount due to the client or amount due by the client.

1. **To calculate the annual income:** To calculate the annual income of the Advocate from the legal profession, it is necessary to maintain proper accounts of his income

from the profession. Maintaining this account is useful for Advocates also. By knowing his Annual Income, he can take steps to improve his profession.

2. **To Calculate income Tax:** Advocates are liable to Pay Income tax for the income derived from the profession. In order to calculate the amount payable as income tax, he has to maintain proper accounts relating to his income and expenditure.To calculate the taxable income, he is entitled to deduct certain expenditure like rent, salary, telephone bill and other administrative expenditure. For this purpose, also he has to maintain proper accounts.
3. **To calculate professional tax:** Every six months the advocates are liable to pay professional tax to the Government. The amount of professional tax varies depending on the income. In order to calculate the amount of professional tax he has to maintain the proper accounts.
4. **To Ascertain the amount due from the client or due to the client:** The account relating to the amount received from the client and the amount received on behalf of the client from others or from the court should be properly maintained. Then only the amount due from the client can be calculated. This will help not only the client but also the Advocate.

PLACE OF KEEPING THE ACCOUNTS BOOKS.

The accounts books and documents relating to the accounts should be kept and maintained by the advocate,

i. At his office.
ii. Where he is carrying on the profession more than one office, then at his head office. But accounts can also be

maintained separately for each branch at the respective branch office.

Penalty for not keeping Account Books: A Lawyer who is legally liable to maintain account books, fails to maintain it or fails to retain it for the prescribed period (cash book and ledger-16 years, other books-8 years) is liable to pay penalty ranging from Rs.2000/- to 1,00,000/- (S.271 A).

Bar council Rules relating to accounting

Accounting is an art of recording, classifying and summarizing in a significant manner the event which are financial in character and interpreting the result there of. An Advocate is under a duty to maintain proper accounts of money received from his client and the amount received on behalf of client from others or from the court. The rules relating to such accounting is dealt in rules 25 to 32 of the Bar Council of India Rules 1975.

Rule 25: An advocate should keep the accounts of the client's money entrusted to him. The accounts should show the amounts received from the client, the expenses incurred for him and the debits made on the account of Advocate fees with the respective dates and all other necessary particulars.

Rule 26: Where moneys are received from the client, it should be entered whether the amount have been received for the advocates fees or expenses. Amount received for the expenses shall not be diverted towards Advocates fees without the consent of the client in writing.

Rule 27: Where any amount is received on behalf of his client the fact of such receipt must be intimated to the client as early as possible.

Rule 28: After the completion of the proceeding, the advocate shall be at the liberty to take the settled fee due to hi to the unspent money in his hand.

Rule 29: Where the fee has been left unsettled, the advocate shall take the fees which he is legally entitled from the moneys of the client remaining in his hands, after the completion of the proceeding. The balance shall be returned to the client.

Rule 30: A copy of the client account shall be furnished to him after getting the necessary copying charges from him.

Rule 31: An advocate shall not make any agreements whereby client's funds in his hands are converted into loans to the advocate.

Rule 32: An Advocate shall not lend money to his client for the purpose of conducting the case.

•

Under the Income Tax Act, every lawyer is required to maintain the following books of accounts and other documents to enable the Assessing Officer to calculate his total income (i) cash book (ii) Receipt Voucher (iii) payment voucher (iv) journal (v) ledger. The accounting year is 1st April to 31st March next year.

1. ***Cash book:*** It is the book in which the amount received by the Advocates from the clients and others and the amount spent for the clients are written. This book is useful for the Advocate to know the amount in his hand on each day.
2. ***Receipt Voucher:*** It is the document prepared for recording the receipt of money by cash or cheque. When an Advocate received money from the client, the Advocate has to issue a receipt to the client. Advocate shall maintain receipt books with serially numbered receipt forms in duplicate. The original receipt should be given to the client and the duplicate

shall be retained by the Advocate.

3. ***Payment Voucher:*** Payment vouchers are used to record such payments for which receipts are not obtainable from the person to whom such payments are made. For example, bus fare, auto fare, court fees, stamps, refreshment expenses etc. In such cases the Advocate signature in the payment voucher and the signature of the person to whom payment is made may be obtained.
4. ***Journal:*** Journal is the book of first entry or original entry. In the journal the transactions are recorded in the order of their occurrence. It should contain the following details (i) Date of Transactions (ii) Account to which the transaction relates (iii) Amount to be debited, (iv) Amount to be credited (v) Explanation of the transaction.
5. ***Ledger:*** The transactions recorded in the journal are to be posted to the separate heads of account in another book called as Ledger. In the ledger different pages are allotted to the different heads of accounts. When the journal entries are posted to the concerned heads of account in the ledger, the page number of the ledger should be noted in the journal for easy reference.

Printed by Libri Plureos GmbH in Hamburg,
Germany